TO MY DEAR FRIEND:

_____

FROM:

_____

978-1-5359-3443-5

Published by B&H Publishing Group
Nashville, Tennessee

Cover and interior design by Katherine Hamm
and Jennifer Tucker, with photography by
Amber Tysl and product by Mary & Martha.

1 2 3 4 5 6 7 • 22 21 20 19

(in)courage author
JEN SCHMIDT

Open-Door Living

Easy Ways to Share the Gift of Hospitality

B&H
PUBLISHING GROUP

NASHVILLE, TENNESSEE

The Heart of Hospitality

She found me in the hall and grabbed me in a bear hug.

"Jen, you'll never believe it. Other than my extended family, I haven't invited anyone to our home in years. I'm not a natural hostess, so I created my list of excuses. But then I read your simple encouragement to take one baby step, to extend one simple invitation, to just open my door. For the first time, I did it.

"I'll admit, I nearly canceled multiple times, but I'm so glad I didn't. We had the best evening together! Why have I waited so long? I felt a sense of freedom and connection that I haven't experienced in a long time. We already have another date on the calendar. I'm so excited."

Her face beamed with joy as she experienced the transforming power of what open-door living can do. To be welcomed and included. To find connection and community.

Since you've said yes to this book, hopefully you're already feeling a stirring, a longing to gather and do life together like my sweet friend. We're going to spend a bit of time leaning into the heart of hospitality. But that word "hospitality" is often laced with a whole lot of expectations and anxiety, am I right?

• Does inviting people into your home feel more like inviting judgment of your entertaining skills and stress to your already maxed-out schedule?

• Do you want to welcome others in but get stuck because making food, cleaning, decorating, and facilitating conversation feels impossible—or at least too overwhelming?

I get it. I've been there, too. But what if you had simple ways to overcome those fears and obstacles? What if you leaned into opening your door instead of keeping it closed? What if the how-tos of hosting people in your home didn't have to get in the way of the get-to gift of welcoming people into your heart and pointing them to Christ?

Whether you're a seasoned host looking for renewed inspiration or a nervous newbie not sure where to begin, this book will equip you with tools for simple food prep, cleaning made easy, creating a welcoming ambience with what you already have, and guiding meaningful conversations without a ton of stress.

If we're honest, our biggest barrier to opening the door to others often is ourselves. We stand in our own way, don't we? What will others think? What if they don't like the food

I serve? My home isn't nice enough to invite others. I just don't have time. We cross the line between welcome and worry when we lose sight of the fact that the whole purpose of hospitality is pointing others to Jesus through serving and loving them.

When we create a home where open-door living is a response to who Christ is in our lives, then the love we demonstrate to our guests is a natural overflow of His presence in our own life.

We serve food not to impress others with any culinary expertise (which may never come) but because gathering around the table allows the physical and soul nourishment to intertwine.

We create a welcoming atmosphere in our homes by adding an element or two of beauty to our living area, not because we want to impress the guests that are coming through our door but because we want to bless them with simple gestures that communicate love.

Ultimately, it comes down to knowing the difference between social entertaining and biblical hospitality.

The entertaining host seeks to elevate herself, to make it about her. When the guest

Our homes—
no matter
how imperfect—
are the most
likely location
for changing the
world around us.

arrives, the entertainer announces, "Here I am. Come into my beautiful abode and have the honor of partaking of all the wonderful things I've spent hours getting done for you. Look at this lavish buffet and the intricate décor. How fortunate for you to be here."

Hospitality is different.

Biblical hospitality offers our best to Him first, understanding that our best to others will then fall into place. When the hospitable hostess swings wide the door, all her attention focuses upward and outward: "You're here! I've been waiting for you, just as Christ waited for me. No one is more important today than you, and I'm thrilled you've come. As Christ has welcomed me, so I welcome you."

Extending hospitality is about freely giving of ourselves while granting others the freedom to be themselves. Shifting our focus from us to them removes all unnecessary expectations. No need to worry about what to say or how to act. Just come as you are.

Hospitality, unlike entertaining, treats everyone as a guest of honor rather than grasping at honor for yourself.
Opening your door has nothing to do with the actual setting, the guest list, or the food.

The atmosphere can be exactly the same yet have very different results based on the heart attitude of the one who welcomes.

Truly, friend, our homes—no matter how imperfect—are the most likely location for changing the world around us. Our homes can be the very vehicle used to point others to God's glory as we invite, welcome, and pursue the heart of our guest as Christ first did the same for us.

This isn't about hosting the next greatest dinner party. It's so much deeper than that. It's about cultivating a heart for others, inviting them to gather, and creating an authentic environment where gracious gestures of kindness and generosity are extended so we can love as Jesus did. When my heart aligns with this purpose, the mismatched dishes and my second hand sofa no longer hold me hostage to others' expectations. I step forward with the proper perspective in check knowing the abundance that flows from open-door living.

Over the next few pages, we're going to continue to unpack simple and encouraging ways to cast off any preconceived notions of exhausting and stress filled, to-do lists and embrace the simple gift of an everyday invitation.

As we get started, think about these four practical aspects of hospitality:

• Food

• Cleaning

• Atmosphere

• Connection

Which one of these elements comes easily to you? Write down three things you already enjoy and feel successful in when it comes to opening your home. [Hint: it could be your favorite crowd-pleasing recipe, the simple tidy-up system you already use, or your go-to icebreaker question for getting to know someone.]

Next, which of these things feels like an obstacle to opening your home? Write down the first worry or stumbling block that pops into your mind when you think about hospitality. Ask God to open your heart to new ways of loving others, right where you are with exactly what you have. Journal your prayer here so you can look back and see how lives can be changed—starting with yours!—when you choose to just open the door.

OUR
home
IS

a safe, refreshing haven

a place where everyone is
valued and welcome

a soft place to land

a place where real life happens

a place where guests are comfortable

a place where rest comes easy
and our souls can breathe

a place full of love and laughter,
tears, and hugs

a place where
the doors swing wide open

Mason Jars

I don't remember when or where my love for vintage mason jars began, but nearly every day I find myself reaching for some type of canning jar. They're not only practical and versatile, but considering I'm looking at a beautiful antique aqua jar filled with white hydrangeas right on my kitchen table, I'd say they're quite beautiful as well.

Just a few of the ways I use mason jars on a regular basis:

- Vase for fresh flowers
- Small planters with dirt and succulents
- Candle holders and luminaries
- Hanging lanterns
- Drinking glasses
- Layered small salads
- Layered desserts
- Yogurt parfaits
- Personal apple pies
- Silverware caddy
- Candy centerpiece

recipe

Chocolate Chip Cookie Cheesecake Bars

Ingredients

1 18-ounce roll refrigerated chocolate chip cookie dough
8 ounce package of cream cheese, softened
1 egg
1/2 cup sugar, granulated
1/2 tsp vanilla extract

Directions

1. Preheat oven to 350 degrees.
2. Line an 8 or 9-inch square baking dish with nonstick foil for easy clean up.
3. Beat cream cheese, sugar, egg, and vanilla until smooth.
4. Cut half of the cookie dough and press evenly in bottom of pan to form the crust.
5. Spread cream cheese mixture over the top of cookie dough base.
6. Crumble remaining cookie dough over the top.
7. Bake for 30-35 minutes or until golden brown.
8. Let cool completely before cutting into bars. If you can wait, they cut better after having been chilled. Store in fridge.

Food and Feasting

Whenever I talk to people about why they have a hard time inviting people over, someone always mentions the stress of food.

Do any of these thoughts sound familiar?

I don't know what to serve.

I'm not a good cook.

How will I ever have it all ready at the same time?

It's just too much work.

This is where we need to stop ourselves. Shut off those negative voices. Shut down the doubt and fear. If food is your roadblock to opening the door, then I want you to understand that limitation and learn how to overcome it. The goal is to spend time with your guests, and if you spend the whole time stressed out in the kitchen, it defeats the purpose of cultivating community.

Inviting people over isn't about serving the perfect recipe or impressing anyone with our culinary skills. It's about opening up our lives to love others—and one of those most tangible ways to connect both the physical and spiritual self is to feed them. If we need the perfect role model for this, look to Jesus.

Throughout the New Testament, we see the emphasis He put on gathering at the table, and His table was marked with radical grace. Everyone was welcome to come and be filled.

Sometimes a gathering looks like fancy china and recipe names I can't pronounce, but my first word of encouragement comes in the form of a great, big kiss.

K.I.S.S., that is. This acronym first made popular by the U.S. Navy stands for, "keep it simple, stupid." Since I try to keep the word "stupid" out of my home, I came up with my own version:

Keep It Simple and Sweet (or Salty)

The secret to K.I.S.S. is to start small. When we overthink, overplan, and overstress about opening our door to others, we overwhelm ourselves and often sabotage our intended baby steps before we take them.

Be spontaneous. Invite one friend over for coffee and offer delicious store-bought coffee cake. If you have time to make your favorite homemade recipe, that's wonderful and guests appreciate the extra effort—but don't let that dictate whether you extend an invitation. Even a box cake mix that has been made in your home (a.k.a. homemade).

What is one simple step you can take this week to open your door to a friend or neighbor? Use one of my suggestions or dream up an idea that fits your family and personality. Just remember to Keep It Simple and Sweet!

What fun to think who we could bless this week with a commitment to K.I.S.S.!

You can implement the K.I.S.S. concept in hundreds of ways, but here are a few simple meal-gathering suggestions to get your creative juices flowing:

• Invite your friends or neighbors for a root beer float party or a "Popsicle and Pop-in" time with the kids. It's a great way to meet new families.

• Snow day? Gather the neighbors for a s'mores and hot chocolate party. Summer day? Fire up the grill or serve popcorn while showing an outdoor movie on the side of your house.

• Host a Breakfast for Dinner party. You could even expand on the theme and invite people to come in their coziest or funniest PJs.

• Host a "Build Your Own _____ Bar" meal. Be creative with ice cream, baked potato, burrito, or pizza bars! Bars work well for large groups, and you can share the work and cost by asking guests to bring toppings. You also can try a bruschetta bar or mashed potato bar for fancier occasions.

• Never underestimate the power of the grill. Guests tend to love anything cooked over a fire, from hot dogs to steaks, and if someone else is manning the grill, you'll be freed up to spend a bit more time on sides and dessert.

Opening your door doesn't require you to be a gourmet chef or have the resources to throw an elaborate celebration. All that's required is a willingness to say "yes" to inviting others into your life.

Simple doesn't always mean casual. Sometimes I desire to elevate my ordinary fare with an elegant touch, and I can't think of a better way than to create a beautiful charcuterie board.

"Charcuterie" is a fancy name for a more involved cheese and cracker plate because everything looks more stylish when served on a large, wooden tray.

The traditional charcuterie board includes cured meats and sausages, but grouping any foods around your theme of choice is a fun and versatile way to serve. The possibilities are endless.

Brunch Tray

This tray could feature deviled eggs, Canadian bacon, smoked salmon, quartered clementines, assorted nuts, mini donuts or bagels, assorted fruits, crackers, cheese, and cream cheese.

Traditional Charcuterie Board

Begin by setting out 2-3 bowls for dips, nuts, olives, or bruschetta, then arrange thinly sliced meats and cheeses on the board. I like to create variety by offering something pre-sliced, something I sliced, and something spreadable.

Finally, fill in the space on the board with an assortment of fruits, veggies, crackers, or sliced baguettes. Anything goes.

Anything Goes

Since we know all foods look elegant when displayed on a beautiful board, why not experiment tonight? Forage through your fridge, arrange your finds with an artistic flair, add a sprig of greenery and elevate your family's ordinary everyday feast. It could be Mexican or Italian-themed, hearty hors d'oeuvres, or even leftovers. Have fun creating.

Use brown or white craft paper as a tablecloth for the serving table. Not only does it allow for easy labeling of dishes, but the clean-up is a breeze. When used on a kids' table with a supply of crayons and markers, they'll create their own masterpiece while they eat.

Brown Sugar Baby.

Broccoli AKA Baby Trees

Hot! Hot! Hot!

Chive On

Bacon it Delicious

Everything Better with Bacon

A Well-Stocked Pantry Makes Hosting Easier

As we lean into a lifestyle of open-door living, flexibility becomes a necessity. With a little forethought, planning, and margin, a well-stocked pantry allows for more confidence and security in the kitchen. When main staples are organized and ready, we have less stress about what to serve and more freedom to focus on our guests.

After years of hosting, these are the staples I keep on hand. From this list, mixed with fresh ingredients, I can create 15-20 main dishes, appetizers, and desserts that make eating with friends and family so much simpler. Keep one designated pantry shelf specifically for hosting needs so that key ingredients are always at your fingertips.

Basic Pantry Checklist

Pantry Goods

Salsa and Tortilla Chips
Dried Pasta
Chicken Stock
Canned Tomatoes
Canned Beans (assortment)
Rice
Cans of Cream Soups
Mixed Nuts
Crackers
Dried Fruits
Cake and Brownie Mix
Canned Fruit
Can of Pie filling
Varying sauces (BBQ, Red, Alfredo,
Hot Sauce, Teriyaki, Sweet and
Sour, Pesto)
Jellies, Peanut Butter
Olives
Potatoes

Refrigerated Items

Cheese: block and shredded
Eggs
Hearty Veggies
Phyllo Pastry Puffs (puff pastries)
Store Bought Crescent Rolls
Cream Cheese
Sour Cream
Butter

Frozen Foods

Pizza Dough Ball or Bread Dough
Pie Crusts
Cookie Dough
Cheese
Frozen Fruit
Frozen veggies
Ground Beef
Shredded Chicken

Use mini muffin pans or decorative ice trays to freeze fruits, soda, juice, or punch for ice cubes to avoid watered-down beverages and add a festive touch. Keep lemon and limes on hand to dress up tap or sparkling water, garnish a plate with a slice, or add some to a bowl for a fresh centerpiece.

Simple Meal Ideas

By keeping your menu simple, everyday hospitality allows you to focus on your company and eliminates the panic about what to serve. If you're prepared with a few easy recipes in your repertoire, extending a last-minute invitation will become nearly effortless.

Power Cooking Hour

Whether cooking for my own family or hosting guests, my weekly goal is to spend one hour of concentrated time focusing on prepping as many food items as possible.

The concept of a Power Cooking Hour is simple: set the timer for one hour, then cook, bake, and freeze as much as you can. In one hour of concentrated time, I am able to break down certain kitchen tasks enough that I can get eight easy meals out of that one hour. Use any appliances you have on hand. I use my rice cooker, Crock-Pot, instant pot, grill, oven, and food chopper.

My primary goal in this one hour is to get proteins prepped. Depending on the size of your grill, freezer, and family, grill up to ten pounds of your choice of chicken, beef, or pork. Once cooked, slice, dice, and divide the proteins into individual freezer bags to be used during the week. I also brown 4-8 pounds of ground beef and then separate the ground beef into one or two-pound servings and season them accordingly for upcoming meals.

This eliminates all the frustration of realizing the ground beef for tonight's chili is still frozen solid. By already having the proteins pre-cooked and divided into freezer bags, it can easily be thawed in the microwave for quick meals.

Apply this same principle to baking. In one hour, you can whip up muffins, quick breads, cookie dough, and cake to freeze. With a little forethought, you'll always have special treats to have on hand (if you can avoid eating all the frozen cookie dough).

This power hour principle has not only revolutionized my family's meal time but has also enabled me to welcome last-minute guests without panicking.

EVERYONE LOVES
a Pizza Party!!!

Pretty much wherever you live, whoever you are, whatever your age, you can never go wrong with a pizza party. It can be as simple as take-out pizza boxes on the counter or a big fancy spread outdoors.

Remember, if all else fails... pizza is always the answer!

The Crust paper thin, thick and doughy, or somewhere in between... the perfect crust makes the perfect pizza! Here are some ideas:

- Keep it incredibly simple by using store bought crusts (remember **K.I.S.S.**?)
- Make pizza "boats" on French bread
- Want homemade dough but short on time? Many grocery stores offer their own homemade pizza dough in the deli. The raw dough is sold in dough ball form so that guests can enjoy the process of making their own personal pizza from start to finish.
- Make your own homemade dough! I know it sounds gourmet, but it's one of the easiest doughs to make. If you have a mixer, you can whip it up quicker than you can run to the store.

Ready to try? Here's my tried and true recipe:

Crusty Pizza Dough

ingredients:

1 package active dry yeast

1 cup warm water - 105 degrees (I have never taken the water's temperature. Stick your finger in to gauge temp)

1/2 tsp salt (I love to use garlic salt for variety, and will add various seasonings as well)

1 tsp olive oil (or any oil)

2 1/3 cups - 3 1/2 cups all purpose flour

directions:

1. Dissolve yeast in warm water in warmed bowl.
2. Add salt, olive oil, and 2 1/2 cups flour.
3. Using dough hook, mix for 1 minute.
4. Continuing on low speed, add remaining flour, 1/2 cup at a time, until dough clings to hook and cleans sides of bowl. Kneed on low speed for 2 minutes.
5. Place in greased bowl, turning to grease top.
6. Cover and let rise in warm place until dough has doubled in size (about 1 hour).
7. Punch down.
8. Brush 14-inch pizza pan with oil; sprinkle with cornmeal.
9. Flatten dough on pan, forming a colar around edge to hold filling.
10. Top with desired filings.
11. Bake at 450 degrees for 15-20 minutes. This makes one small 14-inch pizza.

The Sauce   Once you've got the crust, it's time for the sauce.

There's always the basic red sauce, but offering a few different types of sauces allows for fun customization opportunities. Here are a few to try:

- **Pesto** - Make your own fresh or buy it in a jar.
- **BBQ sauce** - Buy your favorite kind and be generous.
- **Alfredo sauce** - Thick, creamy, buttery alfredo...enough said.
- **Hummus** - A great base for a veggie pizza—light, fresh, and healthy.
- **Salsa** - taco pizza, anyone?

The Toppings

I've heard it said that cake without icing is just bread. In that same vein, pizza without a lot of toppings is _____?

- **Cheese**...glorious cheese! Mozzarella and Parmesan are staples, but if you're feeling fancy, try adding ricotta or gouda with a white sauce. Feels like you're in a restaurant...in the comfort of your own home.

- **Meat choices**: I'm all for simple pepperoni and sausage, but if you want to be adventurous, throw in some ham, bacon, or chorizo. Ground beef makes a great taco pizza, and chicken with a BBQ sauce base is delish!

- **Veggie options**: My kids would disagree, but with vegetables there are few things that are off limits. Serve the classics in small bowls for ease: onions, mushrooms, tomatoes, peppers, olives, and spinach. Elevate the ordinary: try pineapple, capers, zucchini, or jalapenos...the options are endless!

Here are twenty simple main dish suggestions that can be prepped in ten minutes (minus necessary cooking time) if your proteins are precooked:

- Chicken Stir Fry

- Beef or Chicken Enchiladas or Burritos

- Simple Chicken Casserole

- Grilled Chicken Salad

- Chicken Tortilla Soup

- Buffalo Chicken Dip

- Simple Chicken Pot Pie

- Chicken Alfredo

- Chili

- Taco Salad

- Taco Dip

- Taco Pizza

- Taco Soup

- Beef or Chicken Nachos

- Sloppy Joes

- Simple Lasagna with No Boil Noodles

- Stuffed Shells

- Shredded Pork with BBQ Sauce

- Stuffed Biscuits

- Spaghetti

Grocery Tip

Buy a fully cooked rotisserie chicken at the grocery to use for countless recipes. While a full chicken is easy to slice and serve, most delis will now do the all work for you and offer the hand-pulled rotisserie chicken already shredded in small bags so you can immediately mix it into your recipe.

Create a simple hospitality notebook with your tried and true, easy recipes, so all the necessary ingredients and directions are at your fingertips. You don't need anything fancy—a three-ring binder works great. While so much of our organization occurs online, I find that going old school with hard copies still works best. Tape or glue the printed recipe to a piece of cardstock and on the back, write the list of ingredients, then slide them into a page protector. Take a cellphone picture of the ingredients, so you'll have it when you're heading to the store. This binder will be a lifeline when you need ideas, plus if you start jotting down notes, including the people you've served the dishes to, it will become a unique memory journal as well.

Dear Jen:

We are in a season of financial difficulty, and while I want to host, I'm nervous about hosting well on a budget.

Let's talk about the elephant in the room. I won't sugarcoat it: hospitality is easier with money. It's easier not having to scour the sales. It's easier not needing to stress about feeding guests on a tight budget. It's easier being able to freely purchase full-price decorative items to spruce up the house. Hosting anything—*really, everything in life*—is easier with money.

But this is equally true: never has my family experienced a sweeter season of sharing our home, our gifts, our time, or the meager offerings we could give than during those years when we were flat broke. Never was I more convinced that circumstances did not determine my peace.

Remember, small is the new big, and stress-free, meaningful hospitality is our goal.

It takes creativity, but you still have so many options when hosting on a budget.

My #1 money-saving food tip requires you to shift your mindset. Instead of planning your menu first, complete with appetizer and main course items purchased at full price, scour the sale ads, search the marked-down produce and meat sections at the grocery store, buy ahead, and adjust your menu plan accordingly. Shop intentionally, and then plan. I can serve large groups of people very well on a budget if I'm willing to be creative. While other people stock up on Black Friday deals, I buy fresh turkeys. That's when grocery stores are in a frenzy to sell their extras, so I swoop in to feed our family and friends for pennies on the dollar.

Leftovers from after-Christmas hams can stretch into multiple meals, too: potato ham chowder; cheese, ham, and egg breakfast casserole; grilled tomato, ham, and cheese sandwiches; navy beans and split pea soup using the ham hock. You can do this!

Wherever an
open table is set
and
my people are
gathered...
I am home.

recipe

2-Ingredient Homemade Sherbet

Yes, it's true. These two ingredients are a party in your mouth, and you pick the winning combination. Start with all peaches or strawberries, but after you've perfected the blend, try mixing and matching all your favorite fruits. There are so many flavors and possibilities!

Ingredients

1 14-ounce can of sweetened condensed milk
16 ounces of your favorite frozen fruit

Directions

1. Add sweetened condensed milk and frozen fruit to blender and combine until smooth and creamy.
2. Serve immediately for a soft serve consistency.
3. Freeze any leftovers and enjoy later.

*Sweetness preferences vary, so begin with ¾ can of sweetened condensed milk and enjoy a taste test before adding the whole can. Our kids always want to add more frozen fruit for extra.

Spuds and Suds

Sometimes having a large group over for dinner can feel overwhelming. As you step into a lifestyle of hospitality, set yourself up for success and don't bother attempting a multi-dish dinner. Instead, offer a "Spuds and Suds" night highlighting a full baked potato bar with as many creative toppings as you want to provide, and then round out the evening with my favorite go-to dessert that everyone enjoys but rarely serves: Root Beer Floats.

The best part about serving baked potatoes is that you can wrap them in foil, bake them ahead of time, and keep them warm in your Crock-Pot so you have no last-minute serving prep. Guests enjoy bringing their favorite toppings (and they can get very creative if you let them). Add in a green salad to round out the "S" theme and you're good to go! (Although "Spuds, Suds, and Salad" just doesn't have the same ring to it.)

We All Scream for Ice Cream

For those wanting to skip straight to a dessert gathering, why not enjoy a good old-fashioned ice cream social? Gather lawn games, ask people to bring their favorite topping or ice cream flavor, and assemble an evening topped with sweetness. Or go for the gold by building the "world's longest" banana split. Purchase a plastic rain gutter for a few dollars and place it on top of your picnic table. Using the gutter as the big bowl, each guest creates their favorite ice cream sundae side by side. Kids love this, and they'll talk about it for years (especially if you're extra generous with the whipped cream and cherries).

Asian Pork Tenderloin

This simple Asian Pork Tenderloin recipe lends just the right hint of flavors and delivers a delicious tenderloin every time.

Preparation time: 5 minutes, Cooking time: 30-40 minutes

Ingredients

1/3 cup light soy sauce

1/4 cup olive oil

1/3 cup brown sugar

2 tablespoons Worcestershire sauce

2 tablespoons lemon juice

1 tablespoon dry mustard

1 1/2 teaspoons pepper

4 garlic cloves, crushed (or minced)

1 1/2 – 2 pounds pork tenderloin

Directions

1. Mix first 8 ingredients together in strong, freezer-safe plastic bag.

2. Place pork tenderloin in freezer bag and seal. Mix or "smoosh" all ingredients together in bag.

3. Refrigerate overnight or place in freezer for future use.

4. When ready to cook:

   For oven: place thawed pork mixture in glass baking dish and bake at 375 degrees for 30-40 minutes or until done.

   For grill: discard liquid, and grill ten minutes per side. (This depends on size of meat. Use a meat thermometer to make sure it's done.)

   For Crock-Pot: place thawed pork mixture in Crock-Pot and cook low for 4+ hours on low or 3 hours on high. If from frozen, cook 6 hours on low or 4.5 on high, and add 1/4 cup of additional liquid to keep moist. Water will work.

C.O.S.T. Recipe Ideas
(Cook Once, Serve Twice
or Three Times)

Here are three delicious options for additional cooked pork:

• Double the recipe for delicious "Take two" ideas. Slice leftover pork, reheat, and place on a warm hoagie bun. Top with provolone cheese for a quick and hot sandwich. Broil the sandwich to melt the cheese if you like. Serve with some fresh vegetables for a well-rounded meal.

• Roll pork, rice, broccoli, and pineapple into large wraps.

• Slice pork and place on mixed salad greens. Top with your favorite dressing for a light and easy meal.

Cleaning and Decluttering

Ever since I first started opening our door to family, friends, and yes, even strangers, this has been the hardest obstacle for me to overcome.

I've always dreamed of a perfectly clean and organized home where everything can be found in its assigned place. I'm still in awe of my friends that seem to have been born with the orderly gene. My mom has it, and somehow our eldest daughter received it, but it must have skipped me.

As a young mom, I believed the notion that our house needed to be deep-cleaned and spotless before anyone came over. Heaven forbid it looked like five children lived here, right? (Even though they did.) Wrong!

A warm and welcoming home where others feel comfortable means different things to each unique woman. Through the years, I have embraced the "good enough" mentality. Not to be used as an excuse, but this perspective gives freedom to focus on what matters most. **Your home needs to be clean and orderly enough that your family and guests know you care about them but not too perfect that they're uncomfortable.** Have you ever walked through a museum with a young child, continually nervous that they might get something dirty or break something?

It's always best to remove clutter, but large baskets can help creatively conceal loose items on short notice.

No home
is
too small
that
one more
can't be
Welcomed.

Why would I purposefully create that environment for my guests? Let's be honest. When you are at someone's house, do you wander into every room? Do you go upstairs and peek around? (If you do, that's another discussion.) Unless you're specifically invited for a housewarming party, that doesn't occur.

Once I realized that my guests only see a very small portion of our home (the front door area, kitchen, family room, and half bathroom), the pressure was off. I didn't worry about the other rooms (which had the lights off and doors closed). I stopped meticulously scrubbing floors before people arrived (and did a cursory spot check to make sure oatmeal wasn't stuck to the floor) because undoubtedly within minutes, the floors were dirty again. Now I only focus on a few main areas (and even then, I've been known to have random boxes stacked in a corner).

One of the goals of your home is to effectively serve you and your guests. Creating a welcoming place will evolve and vary through different chapters in your life, so know it will look different for each person and house.

If you battle perfectionist tendencies in this department and are held hostage by feelings of inadequacies, determine what is "good enough" for you. Remind yourself, "Grace on, guilt off." Slowly loosen control in that area, so that you give yourself room to breathe and enjoy the process. And if you're on the other end of the spectrum and clutter is a constant nemesis, know that with this simple checklist, you can take baby steps toward welcoming others into a space that's not perfect but is cozy and comfortable.

So let's get cleaning.

It's been said that our front door and entryway become the smile of our home. This area welcomes friends, family, and even the postal carrier, so let's make sure we create a friendly and inviting front-door area.

For me, it starts with wiping down the front door and clearing all the miscellaneous clutter. Somehow mess congregates where people enter. If you have space on a front stoop, consider painting a cute wooden chair or bench and setting a basket of flowers on top. You could also hang a wreath on the door (I found mine for five dollars at a yard sale), or perhaps be bold and give the door a fresh, new paint color.

Recently, I spent two hours and $15 on a can of outdoor paint that requires no sanding or priming and updated my old door. You won't believe the difference it makes! It's a lovely minty green, and it makes me so happy every time I approach my home.

LAST MINUTE
Company's Coming
CHECKLIST

Entry Way / Foyer

(Because it's the first area people see, I want to create a warm welcome that shows my guests, "I'm so glad you're here.")

☐ Welcome Message
(I have a big chalkboard that sits by the front door that I use to write a welcome note.)

☐ Wipe down front door if muddy.

☐ Put away shoes, purse, backpacks, diaper bag.

☐ Make room for coats *(if necessary)*.

☐ Sweep floor.

Family Room

☐ Sweep or vacuum.

☐ Clear any miscellaneous clutter (put in laundry basket and bring into bedroom or rooms with closed doors).

☐ Fluff pillows and blankets.

☐ Light candle.

☐ Dust any necessary surfaces.

Kitchen

☐ Hand wash or store dirty dishes in dishwasher.

☐ Clear counters of clutter.
(Since mine congregates here, I put it in a small Rubbermaid box as a short term "solution.")

☐ Wipe down all surfaces.

☐ Clean out sink.

☐ Spot check oven and front of cabinets.

☐ Pull out dishes, cups, serving utensils, silverware, and arrange the eating space before guests arrive.

Bathroom

☐ Quick clean of toilet. Wipe around bowl.

☐ Surface clean counter and mirror.

☐ Empty trash can.

☐ Add additional toilet paper.

☐ Swap out hand towel.

☐ Light candle.

Overnight Guests:
Preparing a Guest Room

With discount hotels on the rise, hosting overnight guests has become a nearly nonexistent occurrence for many. Requests to spend the night at our house have declined (unless they're under the age of twenty-two—that's escalated) and that makes me sad because most of my favorite hospitality memories have occurred around overnight stays. The depth of discussion and meaningful interaction can't be matched. Leisurely conversations can be stretched over late-night dessert and then continued over morning coffee, so when we have the opportunity to welcome an overnight guest, we jump at the chance. Our desire is that our home is always available, even for an overnight stay, Instead of declining a last minute request due to prior commitments, consider instead clearly communicating expectations.

During our son's graduation weekend, a couple offered their guest rooms to us so our family wouldn't have to stay in an expensive hotel. It was such a kind gesture, and they let us know ahead of time that they would not be home when we arrived. When we got to their house, our hosts had a welcome note waiting for us on the kitchen counter with all the necessary details we might need to know about their house: directions on where to find extra snacks, how to work the coffee pot, their wifi password, etc. They texted us a welcome message and again reminded us that they wouldn't be home until after we were already asleep. When we finally saw them the next morning, they were apologetic for not greeting us, but I assured them their hospitality spoke volumes to us in all the small, thoughtful details. We were aware of their prior obligations, so expectations had been clearly set. They offered hospitality through their home, even when most would have said, "No, we're sorry. We won't be there." I'm so thankful they used their home as a vehicle to serve our family.

Over the years, I've stayed in tiny guest rooms where the simple touches my host included mimicked a five-star hotel. Think through what makes your stay extra special at a fancy hotel. It doesn't take much extra time to pamper your overnight guest, and if you include even half of these generous gestures, they'll feel like they're staying at the Ritz.

Most likely you won't have to purchase special items. Search your house for warm, cozy, inviting touches that you have elsewhere and relocate them for the duration of their stay. Since we don't have the luxury of a separate guest room, our kids' room is always given to the guests. It's important for me to add a few extra special touches to offset the kids' things.

Give Guests a Special Welcome

• Leave a tray on the bed with fresh flowers, a coffee table book, candle, or essential oils. If you don't have a tray, include a simple flower stem in a vase on the nightstand.

• Make sure the beds are made with clean, fresh linens.

• Extra pillows and blankets allow your guest to choose their preference, plus it gives visual interest to the room. For added comfort, layer a fluffy duvet at the bottom of the bed.

• Weather permitting, crack a window to allow the fresh air to permeate the room before your guest arrives.

• Place a welcome note on the pillow with some chocolate.

• Leave a sound machine or fan to create white noise.

• In the corner of the room, add a small basket with additional books or magazines.

• If you have a picture with your guest, add a framed picture of you to commemorate that special memory.

• Provide a basket of prepackaged snacks and a water bottle or pretty water pitcher and stemmed glassware.

• Include a small light on the nightstand.

• Place a luggage rack in the room. I found a vintage one at the thrift store, and it's been perfect for our guests.

• Since remote controls vary, include instructions on how to use them. Print out a picture of the remote and write the steps on it.

• Inquire ahead of time about movie and TV preferences. Offer those options for times when you're gone.

• Leave a basket of extra toiletries for their use. Possible items include a hair dryer, extra wash cloths, towels, disposable razor, toothbrush and toothpaste, feminine products, deodorant, travel size shampoo and conditioner, Ibuprofen, and a heating pad.

recipe
Perfect Party Pork

When you're feeding a crowd, this one pleases them all. The pop makes it party perfect. Plus, with only five minutes of prep time, you'll have more time at the table, less time at the stove.

C.O.S.T. Ideas

• Serve on warmed hoagie rolls with coleslaw or sliders with cheese and grilled onions

• Nachos, carnitas, tortillas or burrito bowl with all the fixings

• Tamale Casserole

Ingredients

Any size Boston Butt Roast (Pork Shoulder Roast – I recommend 5 to 7 pounds so you'll have extra for additional meals.)
All-Purpose seasoning (or mixture of onion powder, garlic powder, salt and pepper)

2 tablespoons of brown sugar
1 whole, peeled onion, sliced into wedges
2 cans of Root Beer, Coke or Dr. Pepper (your choice)
4 tablespoons of your favorite Bottle of your favorite BBQ sauce

Directions

1. Place roast in slow cooker.
2. Rub seasoning and brown sugar over meat.
3. Add onions on top, then slowly pour soda in slow cooker until roast is covered.
4. Cover and cook on low for eight hours or until meat can easily shred. If meat can't shred easily, keep cooking.
5. Once finished, strain additional fat and excess liquid. Shred pork and enjoy. Serve with BBQ sauce.
6. Optional oven instructions: Follow same directions except place onions in bottom of Dutch oven first, then remaining ingredients. Cook at 300 degrees for minimum of six hours. Turn roast 2-3 times during cooking process.

Easy BBQ Chicken

Ingredients

10 boneless, skinless chicken breasts

2 bottles of BBQ sauce

1 cup of water (omit if you like thicker sauce)

Directions

Add all ingredients into Crock-Pot and cook on high for 3 or low for 6 hours. After it's finished cooking, use two forks to shred. Add more sauce to achieve your favorite consistency. For quicker shredding, put cooked chicken in a Kitchen Aid and beat for a minute or so for perfectly shredded chicken.

C.O.S.T. Ideas

Use this chicken for sandwiches, burritos, soup, BBQ chicken pizza or topped on cheesy nachos.

Atmosphere and Ambience

The reason I'm so intent on reframing how we think about hospitality is that I don't want us to miss the one-on-one potential we set in motion each time we open our door to someone.

When we shatter the image of needing a model home and a model life and replace it with an everyday invitation that begins by simply being the person you already are, walls of comparison begin to fall. By welcoming our guests with whatever resources we've already been given, and assuring them they're welcome just as they are, true community begins to emerge. We create an open-door home full of joy and laughter, where tears belong and where life is celebrated in abundance.

Are you convinced yet that opening both our hearts and doors to others doesn't demand a particular or spectacular dinner or décor? Remember how I mentioned that the atmosphere of two scenarios can be exactly the same yet have very different results, based on the heart attitude of the one who welcomes? With this in mind, I begin any opportunity to share hospitality by reminding myself of the goal: to create a special place where people are valued and accepted so they can encounter Jesus more fully.

It's about pointing others to Him. When my heart is right, I can then turn to creating a warm, welcoming atmosphere with

simple elements of beauty. Sometimes all it takes is looking at our house with fresh eyes and brainstorming new ways to make our house a home.

When we create a home that reflects our personality and not one that attempts to mimic a magazine, we can choose to love the home we have. Glean ideas from magazines and Pinterest, as well as friends whose creativity inspires you, but seek out the blessings already surrounding you. Instead of viewing the imperfections of your home as a limitation, allow it to spark creativity and inspiration. See all the ways

you can repurpose and refresh things you already have. Cultivating a welcoming space doesn't have to take a lot of money, just a little intentionality. And that's something we've all got.

Contentment is the cornerstone for creating the most contagious atmosphere for your guests, so instead of allowing the idea of decorating to overwhelm you, focus on one area to freshen up immediately and just start. Sometimes hosting gives us the simple push to stop procrastinating on small house projects we already want to complete.

Paint

Over and over I'm amazed by how much a simple coat of paint will do. Whether it's repainting a wall or freshening an old piece of furniture, paint packs the biggest punch for your dollar. Our walls are prime real estate in any room and the colors you choose set the tone. A wall can be a simple, neutral backdrop for the furniture and accessories or it can serve as the focal point that creates a big impact. Nothing brings such instant satisfaction like a great before/after paint project.

Spray paint and a metallic paint pen are valuable party tools for decorating. In minutes, I can add festive accents or personalized messages with a flare. Gather mismatched vases, jars, signs, or candleholders and spray paint them to coordinate to your color theme. Without buying any new party supplies, you can elevate your ordinary items.

DIY Chalkboard

My favorite way to greet guests is by personalizing a message on the huge chalkboard I made for less than $10. And it's so easy to do.

At the thrift store, purchase the largest framed picture you can find. Only concern yourself with the size and frame and not the art. Spray paint the frame if you don't like the color and then paint over the actual picture with chalkboard paint. Voila! It's sure to become a favorite.

Now you can greet every guest with a warm, personalized welcome. In between visitors, write "I love my family" as a special reminder.

Shop Your House

Enjoy a treasure hunt in your own space with eyes that see fresh possibilities in your old items. When you challenge yourself to think outside the box, you can breathe new life into something ordinary.

If guests are coming for a short time, focus on where they'll gather most. For me, it's always the kitchen and family room, so I add a few elements of beauty to each spot. Remember, K.I.S.S.—keep it simple and sweet.

Thrift Store Finds

I truly believe that if Jesus walked the earth today, He would hang out with me at our local thrift store. If He can heal the blind and make the lame walk, surely He can surprise me by turning someone else's trash into my treasure, and He does it—time and time again.

The majority of the photos in this book showcase my friend and photographer, Amber's home, as well as my own.

The kitchen tables, chairs, dishes, baskets, frames, lamps, plant stands, mason jars, vases, chandeliers (and more) are just a few items that we repurposed. You'll find them all scattered throughout the book.

Look Outside

God is the master decorator. Not only do the heavens declare the glory of God, but the whole world is His masterpiece, so let's take decorating lessons from His creation.

Take cues from the naturally occurring colors and elements. After you finish finding treasures in your own home, shop your yard, the neighbor's yard (with their permission, of course), or your local grocery. Add blooming flowers or greenery to glass bottles, wooden bowls, vases, pots, or any unique object. Bring elements from outdoors inside. Every gathering area benefits from bringing outdoor elements in.

Cozy Up the Living Space

"Your home is so cozy" is one of the best compliments a host can hear. Since I go for the "open-door, open-fridge, comfy-sofa, invitation into the presence of Christ" kind of welcome, this communicates that my guests feel at home. Though we all have different decorating styles—whether that be French country, shabby chic, eclectic, formal, contemporary, or minimalist—style should never diminish a room's comfort.

Layer, Layer, Layer

Varying textures, colors, and patterns will warm up a sterile room in minutes.

One of the easiest ways to instantly cozy up a gathering area is by mixing textures on sofas and chairs. Think outside the box. Table runners, throws, quilts, vintage tablecloths, rugs, coverlets, and fabric samples can all be used.

If you're struggling with the appearance of your furniture (ours leans toward the well-loved, a.k.a. old and worn out, side), don't let that discourage you. Use fuzzy throws to spruce up old furniture. I draped a beautiful blanket over the edge of our worn club chair, disguising a ripped corner. Then by layering a simple, white chenille bedspread over our dated brown sofa and adding a pop of color with a few fun, accent pillows, I turned an outdated corner into a cute, cozy gathering spot to freshen up our room.

Focal Wall

If a big, blank wall is your stumbling block, incorporate a fine design element into your own home without the high-end price tag. Large art makes a huge impact, so an amazing solution is to frame a large, beautiful piece of fabric. So many gorgeous sample patterns are available to bring warmth to the room, but maybe you have an heirloom piece tucked away. Grandma's quilt, a piece of your wedding dress, or a shirt with sentimental memories can all become memorable art for your living room.

Another secret for creating impactful art is repetition. If you don't have one large piece, use several frames in the same size and include pieces of art such as fabric, scrapbook paper, maps, architectural drawings, wallpaper, children's artwork, natural elements, or photos to create a focal wall

For celebrations pick one focal wall (inside or out) and maximize decorations in that space. Do it up big in one spot. Some of my favorite choices include:

- Balloon wall
- Fabric buntings
- Streamers
- Hanging lanterns
- Beach balls

Dining by Candlelight

Create an experience that reminds your family and guests that actions speak louder than words. When is the last time you ate dinner by candlelight? Do you remember the tone it set? How those flickering lights helped soothe your soul?

Whether it's frozen pizza or pasta, salad or sirloin, eating by candlelight is one of our family's favorite things to do. It allows the hectic pace of the day to fizzle and conversation to flow gracefully. It also creates a beautiful, calm atmosphere—even on those days or weeks when calm is the furthest thing from reality, and laundry is piled on the sofa. Even if we're eating mac and cheese on paper plates, we still turn off the overhead lights and eat by candlelight every time we gather as a family.

Candlelit dinners have become a tradition for my family, and it's flowed over to all my hosting opportunities as well. Nothing can beat the beautiful ambience that candlelight offers; the small act of lighting a candle can soothe the soul.

Lighting

Soft lighting is always preferred over a big, overhead light. If your gathering room is too dark, add a small lamp to a side table.

White lights and candles make everything magical, so use them liberally. Candles cultivate beauty, so scatter unscented votive candles on the table or group tapered candles of varying heights. String white lights on trees or line the walkway with lanterns and torches.

Evening outdoor lighting hack:

Spray paint basic hoola hoops silver or gold and then wind white lights around each hoop. Hang them from trees or fences for a beautifully, unique backdrop

Simple Tablescape

Don't let that fancy word fool you. It's simply an arrangement of your favorite items gathered on the table (or island, mantle, dresser, picnic table, or side table). Use what you already have on hand and get your creative juices flowing. Based on what you assemble, a tablescape helps set the tone for your gathering. Items you might use include:

• Photo frames, or mirrors

• Fabrics, pretty napkins, doilies, quilts, or throws

• Flowers or foliage

• Fresh fruit

• Baskets, books (to give height), or candles

• Tea trays, vases, or bowls

• Mismatched glassware or serving pieces of similar color.

• Cake stands and trays offer style and functionality. Group and layer decorative or similar food items together on a tray or pedestal for an organized, clean look. When you need to clear space on the table, you can simply remove the entire tray. It couldn't be easier to ready your table for use.

The Table Runner Secret

One of my best party tricks must stay a secret between you and me. My table runner for the Burrito Bar? It's wrapping paper. No one ever knows, and it's been my go-to trick for dozens of gatherings and events over the last few years. There are so many gorgeous options for wrapping paper, from majestic metallics to playful prints, and it can be used to layer and add an impact in a variety of ways.

Tasked with decorating a sterile school cafeteria with two-day notice and no budget, I knew this would be the perfect option. After finding a combination of white table cloths, sheets, and cloth curtains to cover the table, I then created beautiful runners in school colors using wrapping paper and burlap.

When I topped the tables with votive candles and bud bases filled with fresh flowers, the plain lunch room transformed into a dazzling candlelit affair with none the wiser.

Yes, the Lord cares about our simplest of details, even decorations on a budget.

Have fun and think outside the box. These layered "tablecloths" are actually two bed skirts. Aren't they darling?

Engage the Senses

Stimulating the senses is a wonderful way we experience life, as well as communicate love in simple ways to our family and guests. Think of all the memories our senses provoke. We can taste a favorite meal and instantly be back in Grandma's kitchen. Senses hold strong triggers, so as we welcome family and guests, think through each of the five senses.

Smell: What can you do right now to make your house smell homey? Open the window to let the fresh air inside. Simmer apple peels with cinnamon on the stove or pop cookies in the oven. Bake homemade bread or buy frozen rise-and-bake loaves. Diffuse essential oils or light a scented candle. Hang your sheets outside to dry and let that fresh air scent lull your guests to a great night's sleep. Create a beverage station so guests have instant access to coffee (my favorite smell of all).

Sight: Bring beauty into your home. Grab a mason jar and fill it with cut flowers, foliage, and flowering sticks from outside. Light a candle, and let the soft glow make a messy counter more manageable. Fill a pretty bowl full of fresh, colorful fruit. Print a new family picture and display it proudly.

Touch: Add a new, soft hand towel or soft rug to the guest bathroom. Go out of your way to greet your family with a big hug. Fluff some pillows, add soft blankets to sofas and beds, and then take a few minutes to turn down the sheets. Surprise loved ones and tuck them in at night. Lay your hands on them and pray a blessing over them.

Sound: When guests arrive, set the mood and fill the silence with a playlist that reflects the atmosphere of your gathering. Play jazz, oldies, dance music, or praise songs in the background. If weather permits, open a window to enjoy the sounds of nature.

Taste: Remember, it's not what you serve but how you serve. Gather and feed. The rest falls into place.

Tea Time

Taking tea together reminds us to mimic Jesus' pace. He was never too busy. He was never in a hurry. Jesus carved time into His schedule and viewed interruptions as invitations. Slow down and savor a cup of tea or coffee. There's life-giving beauty when we embrace simplicity and prioritize people over productivity.

The Party Box

With a few key hospitality pieces you can easily elevate an ordinary paper plate mentality to something special. Over the years, I've invested in timeless statement pieces, but I'm continually on the hunt for unique party decor. When I find them on sale, I store them in my hospitality hutch for easy access. Start small. Create one designated shelf (or box or cabinet) so you're always ready.

For the unique items I don't use regularly, I've dubbed a Rubbermaid container as "The Party Box," which I share with others. When you're intentional about buying things on sale, you don't have the stress of paying full price in the planning process. Shop after holidays and buy items that aren't holiday specific at deep discount. Pastel Easter colors can be used for women's gatherings, while silver and gold items found after Christmas are perfect throughout the year.

Hospitality Décor Essentials

- Candle holders
- Votive candle holders
- Serving bowls
- Tablecloths (new or vintage)
- Table runner
- Cloth napkins
- Cake stand
- Glass bowls
- Pedestals
- Tiered tray
- Wooden serving tray
- Water pitcher
- White dishes to mix and match with color
- Lanterns

Tip
I always make extra soup to freeze.
Not only is it better the next day
after the flavors meld, but those
leftovers can be used as the main
topping for your baked potato bar
and can be drizzled over tortilla
chips for some gourmet nachos
in minutes.

recipe

Dump and Run Taco Soup

Preparation time: 5 – 10 minutes

This recipe may also be made in a Crock-Pot. Just dump all the ingredients in the morning (only with cooked taco meat option), run your errands, and let it cook all day. If you have it on low, you can easily cook it for 6-8 hours. If you put it on high, cook for 3 hours and then turn to low. Since all the meat is cooked, it's just about heating thoroughly and letting flavors meld.

Ingredients

2 pounds ground beef
1 small onion (optional)
2 garlic cloves (optional)
1 package of taco seasoning
1 1/2 cups water
2 – 15 ounce cans undrained beans, your choice (I typically use black beans and pintos, but great northern, ranch style, or mild chili beans are all great options.)

1 small bag of frozen corn or 15-ounce can whole kernel corn, drained
1 14-ounce can stewed tomatoes
1 can diced tomatoes with green chiles
1 14-ounce can chopped green chiles (optional)
1 package of dry ranch salad dressing mix
Cheese, tortilla chips, sour cream (optional garnishes)

Directions

1. In large pot or dutch oven, fry ground beef, chopped onion, and minced garlic. Drain grease.
2. Add taco seasoning into beef mixture and mix well.
3. Stir in the remaining ingredients.
4. Bring to a boil and reduce heat.
5. Simmer uncovered for 15 minutes or until heated through, stirring occasionally. The more time it has to simmer, the deeper the flavors.
6. If you prefer "soupier" consistency, add a bit more water.
*As pictured here, you may substitute precooked, shredded chicken for the beef.

Easy Chicken Divan

This Easy Chicken Divan takes the classic recipe but cuts the prep time in half. Preparation time: 10 minutes, Cooking time: 40 minutes

Ingredients

2 10-ounce packages frozen broccoli spears
6 boneless, skinless chicken breasts
Seasoning salt, pepper
2 10-3/4 ounce cans cream of chicken soup (can substitute other cream soups)

1/2 cup shredded sharp cheddar cheese
1/2 cup mayo
1/2 teaspoon curry powder
1/2 cup fine, dry breadcrumbs
2 tablespoons butter, melted

Directions

1. Preheat oven to 350 degrees.
2. Cook broccoli in microwave according to package.
3. While broccoli is cooking in microwave begin sauce.
4. Combine soup and next 3 ingredients in saucepan.
5. Cook over medium heat, stirring constantly until the cheese melts.
6. When broccoli is finished, place in a greased 9 × 13 baking dish and top with chicken. Liberally salt and pepper chicken breast. (I use a basic seasoning salt or garlic salt.)
7. Pour sauce over chicken and broccoli.
8. Sprinkle with breadcrumbs and drizzle butter over breadcrumbs.
9. Bake, uncovered for 40 minutes or until chicken is done. (Check at 30 minutes by cutting a small slice in the middle of one of the chicken breasts.)

Conversation and Community

So here's where we stand. Our home is relatively picked up, simple foods are ready to be offered, the ambience has been set, and we're excited to create community.

Once the doorbell rings, the fun really starts. It's time to welcome your guests, making them feel valued, included, and loved. It's your time to enjoy friends—old and new—while helping them feel at home.

But after all this, what if the conversation starts to falter?

Many women have shared their fears with me about hosting, especially in terms of how to facilitate conversation. I understand that's a real concern, and for many, it signifies stepping completely out of your comfort zone. Yet just as you can learn to become more comfortable with opening your door over time, I promise this too is a skill you can learn.

When you feel anxious over what to talk about, remember that at the core, we all desire to feel seen and heard. So don't overthink this.

You don't have to create a "life of the party" persona. Be as hospitable as you can; exactly as the Lord has made you.

The most gracious hosts begin by showing interest in their guests, knowing how to ask good questions and learning

to listen well. That is something we can all do. Intentionally set a safe "table" for open conversations to flow, then allow the Lord to steer you with both a generous spirit and wisdom to facilitate effectively.

As guests begin to arrive, those first few minutes are some of the most challenging. There can be awkward moments when maybe the food's not quite ready, you're still waiting for more people to arrive, or there's exhausting small talk to push through. For that very reason, this is the most important time to ensure guests feel welcomed and relaxed. Hosts help set the tone for a gathering. Take that baby step forward with confidence and know without a doubt that God choose you to make a difference in the life of your guests. You've been called to champion His love through open door living.

So what does this look like?

For me, when the doorbell rings, I'm typically involved with last-minute preparations. So how do I address that tension? It really varies depending on the group of guests arriving, but often, the way to make most arrivals feel welcome is by not being TOO ready. If my goal is to welcome guests and make them feel at home right away, I'll invite them into the kitchen where I'm working. Rather than

making them stand idly by, I'll agree to let them help if they offer. Something simple like filling the water glasses may give them a sense of belonging. Since I view biblical hospitality as a lifelong process and not a one and done event, my desire is that guests feel included in my everyday life. Welcoming their last-minute help puts guests at ease, reminds them my life isn't perfect, and gives them a sense of purpose.

For those who naturally have everything done before guests arrive, that's great, too. Through my decades of open-door living, I'm convinced there is no one right way to practice hospitality. It will look different in every situation, so assess your environment and do what works best for you. Just know that your most important goal when the doorbell rings is to extend a warm welcome.

Part of being a gracious and intentional hostess includes making thoughtful introductions. When guests don't know each other, be intentional in the process. Avoid introductions that put too much emphasis on a person's career or what someone does, and instead mention common interests or shared experiences, such as travel, sports, volunteer activities, church affiliations, or favorite books or shows. People identify closely with places they've called "home," so using locations or home cities is another way to begin connecting guests in a more personal way. It may be as simple as introducing guests with how you first met them and allow shared history to spark new conversations.

Throughout the gathering be mindful of anyone standing alone or not included in conversations. We can all remember a time when we've been the lonely, new girl waiting for an invitation to the inner circle or even a word of welcome. What an honor that we get to be the difference and change all that. As either a host or guest, we can be a lifeline of kindness for someone else, so be sensitive to those needs and come to their rescue.

The heart of biblical hospitality is to love and serve God and others. I can't think of a better way to do that than making time and space to really get to know someone, and it can simply begin by asking questions.

Asking questions shows humility. It means you want the focus directed at others and not on yourself. Questions give everyone a voice. As a host, you'll find the trickiest part is learning to graciously interrupt those that tend to monopolize the time and steer the conversation so that everyone is included.

The best way to facilitate this is to have a few conversation-starter questions ready. Make sure they're open-ended questions. Yes-or-no questions are immediate conversation killers. For years, I've had a jar of 200 questions that sits on our table. Even among our family, we always enjoy diverse discussions that we'd never naturally gravitate toward without the extra help of "the jar."

It might feel a little strange at first—I get it. But it's okay to be honest and start out by saying, "This may seem like forced bonding, but I promise, it's a fun way to get to know each other. You won't regret it."

Begin with some of the conversation starters we've provided and use them to start your own conversation jar. Write them out on cute note cards, and put them at each place setting on your table or put them in a jar in the center like I do.

If a guest answers with brevity, I've learned to urge people to continue by saying, "That's so interesting. I'd love to hear more." Or, "Can you elaborate on that? What did you learn from . . . ? How did you feel when. . . ?" This keeps the conversation going and lets your guests know you're still engaged. As I listen to them share, I take note of things left unsaid. Did they start to go into further detail, but something held them back? Is there a way that I can make them more comfortable to open up?

Part of your role as host is creating a safe place for guests to share deeper and more authentically. This doesn't necessarily occur with only one gathering, but as you pursue hospitality from that deep, spiritual well that's filled only by Him, you realize that vulnerability in conversation serves as the truest gateway to community, as well as to real and abiding friendships.

Some of you may feel comfortable opening your home but not with the hosting duties. Ask a friend who facilitates conversations easily to host with you and help direct the flow of the evening. There's nothing wrong with asking. If you're willing and ready to take the first step, deeper relationships will develop as you get out of your comfort zone. By depending on God, you'll discover He even cares about things like meaningful conversations and will help you grow in leading them.

When we put listening to someone's story at the top of our agenda, we not only take pressure off ourselves to host a perfect event, but we are able to focus on what really matters—the people in front of us and creating a community that cares.

After all, connecting with others so we can love them well—in a tangible way—is a foundational for open-door living.

The heart of biblical hospitality is to love and serve God and others.

Conversation Starters

• If you could visit any place in the world, where would you go? What would you do there? What's your favorite place you've already visited?

• What chore did you dislike when you were a child? What about now? Any chores you enjoy?

• If you could only eat three foods for the rest of your life, what would they be?

• If you could have dinner with anyone from history, who would it be and why? Who would you like to meet who's still alive?

• How would you describe yourself to someone who has never met you?

• Describe your perfect day, from when you'd first wake up until you'd go to sleep.

• Where did you grow up? Share a favorite childhood memory from that place.

• If you won $20,000 and couldn't use it to pay bills, what would you buy for yourself?

• If you could ask God one question right now, what would it be?

• Do you have a faith background? If you do, tell us a bit about your church history.

• Describe how you'd like your life to be five years from now. Ten years from now.

• What is one thing that makes you really happy? What about incredibly sad? When's the last time you cried and why? When's the last time you laughed super hard and why?

recipe

Easy Ravioli Bake

This deliciously easy meal is the best in homemade comfort food without all the work. Preparation time: 5 minutes, Cooking time: 55-65 minutes

Ingredients

1 jar (26 – 28 ounces) tomato pasta sauce
1 package (25 – 27 ounces) frozen cheese-filled ravioli
2 tablespoons grated Parmesan cheese
2 cups shredded mozzarella cheese
Diced onions, peppers, olives, mushrooms, or even spinach (optional)
Italian seasoning (optional)

Directions

1. Preheat oven to 350 degrees.
2. Spray bottom of 9 x 13 pan with cooking spray.
3. Spread 3/4 cup of the pasta sauce on bottom of baking dish.
4. Arrange half of the frozen ravioli in single layer over sauce. Top with half of the remaining pasta sauce and then optional veggies. If sauce needs more seasoning, sprinkle Italian seasoning now. Top with 1 cup of the mozzarella cheese.
5. Repeat layers once, starting with ravioli. Sprinkle with Parmesan cheese.
6. Cover with aluminum foil and bake 40 minutes. Remove foil; bake uncovered for 15 more minutes, or until cheese has melted and center is hot. Let stand 10 minutes before cutting.

recipe

Citrus Herb Chicken

This fresh, tangy dish is packed with unexpected flavors.
Preparation time: 10 minutes, Cooking time: 35-40 minutes.

Ingredients

6 boneless skinless chicken breasts

Salt and pepper

3 tablespoons lemon, lime, or orange juice

2 teaspoons garlic salt

2 teaspoons dried oregano (crushed)

1 teaspoon chili powder

1/4 teaspoon pepper

Lemon herb seasoning (optional)

Directions

1. Preheat oven to 425 degrees.
2. Rinse chicken and pat dry.
3. Lay the chicken in even layer in pan.
4. Lightly salt and pepper the top.
5. Drizzle with juice.
6. Combine oregano, chili powder, garlic salt, and pepper.
7. Rub seasoning mixture into chicken, turning the pieces to coat evenly.
8. Lightly sprinkle a bit of Lemon Herb seasoning over everything. (optional)
9. Bake for 35-40 minutes (until the chicken is tender and juices run clear). This is also delicious cooked on the grill. If you have difficulty telling if chicken is done, your meat thermometer should read 170° for breasts and 180° for legs or thighs.
10. Spoon the extra pan juices over the chicken before serving.

C.O.S.T. Tip
• Slice into chicken strips for a delicious salad.
• Create a restaurant-quality Greek pita. Add chicken, cucumbers, tomatoes, romaine lettuce or alfalfa sprouts, red onion, feta (or your choice of cheese), and a dab of Greek yogurt or dressing for a fresh menu option.

Closing

There's nothing like the life-giving gift of invitation. Trust me, God will surprise you. He delights to bring good things to His people, and He often does this through gathering together.

Living a life of welcome becomes easier and easier the more we do it, so I hope my encouragement to start right where you are, with exactly how God made you, inspires all of us to fling those doors wide open.

I can't wait for us to look back in one year, five years, twenty-five years, and glimpse the transforming power of what open-door living can do in and through the lives of people who step forward and decide, "I'm willing and available." That declaration changes everything.

Just open the door.

Come on in!

Hospitality is one of the best ways to live out the two greatest commandments: Loving *God* with all your heart and loving your *neighbor* as yourself.

*Resources to help you change
the world around you,
one open door at a time.*

Book
justopenthedoor.com

Bible Study
lifeway.com/justopenthedoor

VIDEO-BASED
7-SESSION BIBLE STUDY

A Study of Biblical Hospitality

Just Open the Door

BIBLE STUDY

(in)courage author
JEN SCHMIDT

Just Open the Door

Invitation Can Change a Generation

Jen Schmidt

FOR THE LAST DECADE, Jen Schmidt has been encouraging, challenging, and cheering on women to embrace both the beauty and bedlam of their everyday lives on her popular lifestyle blog, *Balancing Beauty and Bedlam*.

A popular speaker, worship leader, and founder/host of the annual Becoming Conference, Jen shares with humor and authenticity as she invites others to join her on this bumpy, beautiful life journey.

She lives in North Carolina with her husband, five children, a few too many animals, and an available sofa for anyone who needs it.

beautyandbedlam.com Jenschmidt_beautyandbedlam
 facebook.com/beautyandbedlam @beautyandbedlam

(in)courage

TO SAY WE LOVE COMMUNITY might be an understatement.

At (in)courage, our hearts beat for strong, healthy, God-honoring friendship. Nothing brings us more joy than watching like-hearted women connect.

Connecting with others lightens the load and adds space for more laughter — and healing — because we know we aren't alone.

www.incourage.me   @incourage